Children
of the
INDIAN BOARDING SCHOOLS

Children
of the
INDIAN BOARDING SCHOOLS

Holly Littlefield

PICTURE
the
AMERICAN
PAST

Carolrhoda Books, Inc./Minneapolis

Front cover: Albuquerque Indian School, about 1895. The boarding schools tried to teach Indian children to be loyal to the United States rather than to their own nations.
Back cover: Phoenix Indian School. Most schools required children to practice the Christian religion.
Page one: Phoenix. A boy paints a classmate in a traditional European style.
Page two: Pierre Indian School. Girls play croquet during a break from classes and chores.
Opposite page: Haskell Institute, 1914. The school's football team takes the field.

Special thanks to Brenda J. Child, Associate Professor of American Studies at the University of Minnesota, for her invaluable assistance in reviewing the manuscript. Thanks also to Shannon Zemlicka for caring about every detail—H. L.

Editor's note: Every effort has been made to specify the nation or tribal membership of the individuals pictured and quoted in this book. In some cases, this information was not available.

Carolrhoda Books, Inc.
A division of Lerner Publishing Group
241 First Avenue North
Minneapolis, MN 55401 U.S.A.

Website address: www.lernerbooks.com

LIBRARY OF CONGRESS CATALOGING-IN-PUBLICATION DATA

Littlefield, Holly, 1963–
    Children of the Indian boarding schools / Holly Littlefield.
      p.   cm. — (Picture the American past)
    Includes bibliographical references and index.
    ISBN 1-57505-467-1 (lib. bdg. : alk. paper)
    1. Off-reservation boarding schools—United States—History—Juvenile literature. 2. Indian children—Education—United States—Juvenile literature. 3. Indian children—Cultural assimilation—United States—Juvenile literature. [1. Off-reservation boarding schools. 2. Indians, Treatment of. 3. Indians of North America—Education.] I. Title. II. Series.
E97.5.L57 2001
371.829'97—dc21   00-009456

Manufactured in the United States of America
1 2 3 4 5 6 – JR – 06 05 04 03 02 01

Contents

In 1876, a Cheyenne warrior named Howling Wolf created this painting of his nation's first meeting with European Americans. Howling Wolf was a prisoner at an American fort led by Richard Henry Pratt, who later founded Carlisle Indian Industrial School.

School Away from Home

*When I was about 8 years old the soldiers came and rounded
up as many of the Blackfeet children as they could.
The government had decided we were to get
White Man's education by force.*
—Lone Wolf, a Blackfeet
boarding school student

In the 1400s and 1500s, millions of people lived on the land
that came to be called North America. These Native Americans
belonged to many nations and tribes. Each group had its own
government, language, traditions, and way of life.

Then Europeans came to explore and take the land. The first
explorers believed they were in the Indies, so they called the people they met Indians. Like the Indians, the Europeans had their
own languages and traditions. Most Europeans did not respect
the Indians' ways. They believed their own ways were better.
They also believed the land should be theirs to settle and use.

Many more Europeans came to North America. They began to push the Indians off the land. Their descendants, the European Americans, did the same. Many Indians fought to keep their homes, and many died. By the 1800s, most Indian nations had agreed to sign treaties with the American government. The Indians had to move onto small portions of land called reservations. In exchange for land and peace, the American government made promises. They would give the Indians money, food, and education for their children. Most of these promises were not kept.

Lakota leaders signed a treaty with the United States in 1868. A few years later, Americans broke their government's promise that the Lakota could keep the Black Hills forever.

These children, shown in about 1873 at their home in what later became Oklahoma, are believed to be Wichita Indians.

Life on the reservations was hard. The Indians struggled to make a living on their reduced lands. Most families were poor. Many European Americans believed that the Indians would be better off if they gave up their traditions. They should speak English, become Christian, and farm the land as European Americans did. So in the early 1800s, Christian churches began to open mission schools on the reservations. The purpose of these schools was to teach Indian children to live like European Americans.

Some European Americans thought the reservation schools did not go far enough. An army officer named Richard Henry Pratt believed that Indian children should be taken away from their families. Far from home, children could be taught or forced to accept a new way of life. Pratt convinced the government to build a boarding school. At this school, Indian children would live with European American teachers for many years. In 1879, the Carlisle Indian Industrial School opened in Pennsylvania.

Carlisle, 1882. Richard Henry Pratt (back row) with a group of Navajo children who had just arrived at the school

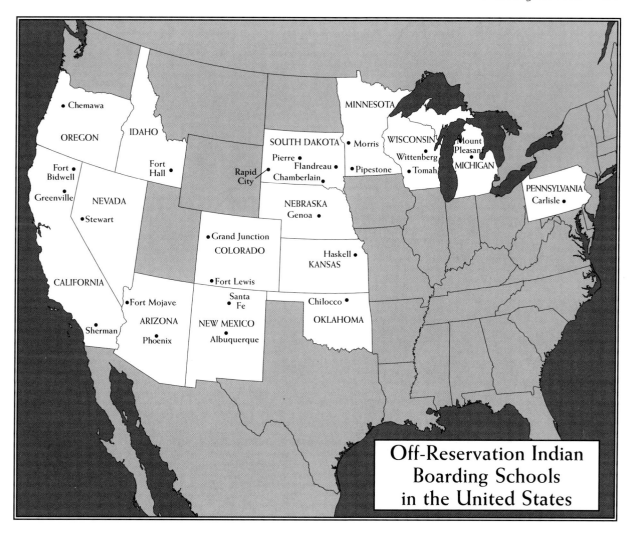

Off-Reservation Indian Boarding Schools in the United States

In the 1880s and 1890s, dozens of other boarding schools opened. Some were on or near reservations. Others were hundreds of miles away.

Albert Hensley, a Winnebago who attended Carlisle, brings his two daughters and two nieces to a boarding school in about 1915.

Some parents agreed to send their children to boarding school. They believed that the children needed to learn English and new job skills. Other families sent children because they could not afford to feed them. Frank Mitchell, a Navajo boy, found "plenty to eat [at school], more food than I used to get at home. I was willing to go to school if they were going to feed me."

Other parents refused to send their children. Sometimes the government took them anyway. Lone Wolf, a Blackfeet boy, was eight when soldiers forced him from his family. "Oh, we cried for this was the first time we were to be separated from our parents," he remembered. Thousands of Indian children were taken from their homes and sent away to an unknown future.

These Hopi leaders chose to go to prison rather than send their children to a boarding school. They were held at Alcatraz Island for seven months in 1895.

Below: Chauncey, Henry, and Richard after school officials changed their clothing and hairstyles

Above: Carlisle, about 1883. Three Lakota boys—Richard Yellow Robe, Henry Standing Bear, and Chauncey Yellow Robe—upon their arrival

LEARNING NEW WAYS

I don't want to stay here . . . . Come after me please,
papa, I am so lonesome for home.
—from a letter by Nora Cailis, who attended a
boarding school in Oklahoma

New students usually did not receive a warm welcome at boarding school. Instead, teachers began to make them look like European American children. Native clothing was taken away and replaced with uniforms. The children's hair was usually cut short. Gertrude Simmons, an eight-year-old Dakota girl, remembered having her hair cut at White's Manual Labor Institute in Indiana. "I cried aloud, shaking my head all the while until I felt the cold blades of the scissors against my neck."

The children's names were also taken away. Each student was given an English name instead. At Carlisle, a Brulé Lakota boy called Ota Kte was renamed Luther Standing Bear. At Grand Junction Indian School in Colorado, a Navajo boy was renamed Rip Van Winkle. John Rogers, an Ojibwe, remembered that "we all had to go by the names that had been given us . . . but among ourselves . . . we would still call each other by our Indian names."

Carlisle. In the Lakota language, Anpetu Waste's name meant "Pretty Day." At school, she was renamed Anna Laura.

Pierre, about 1898. Students practice writing English.

Many children did not know English when they arrived at school. But they were not allowed to use their own languages. Children who spoke any Native language might be given extra chores, locked up, or beaten. At one school, students who were caught speaking Kiowa were forced to brush their teeth with lye soap until their mouths were raw and bleeding. Still, many students continued to secretly speak their own language with friends and siblings. At Flandreau Indian Boarding School, Ojibwe children even learned some Dakota words from their classmates.

Most schools required students to go to long church services and celebrate Christian holidays. Indian spiritual traditions and practices were forbidden. Some children adopted the Christian religion. Others just pretended. An Ojibwe boy named Basil Johnston attended a boarding school in Ontario, Canada. He remembered how his friends made a joke of saying grace before breakfast. "Bless this mush," they whispered. "I hope it doesn't kill us."

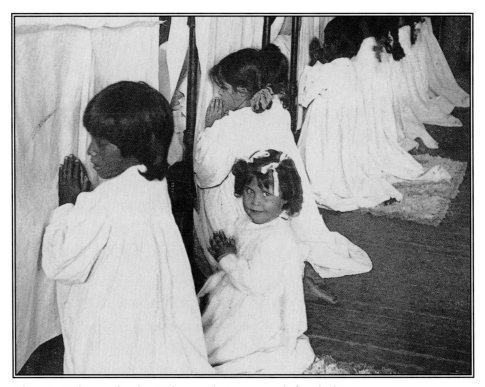

Phoenix Indian School. Girls say their prayers before bedtime.

Albuquerque Indian School, about 1895. Military-style uniforms and American flags were part of the program for these boys.

One goal of the boarding schools was to teach Indian children to follow orders. So most schools were run like military camps. Students learned to march in line and do military drills. A Riverside Indian School student remembered, "We marched everywhere, to the dining hall, to classes; everything we did was in military fashion."

Carlisle. Children work at a chalkboard under a teacher's watchful eye.

On weekdays, the children went to class. They learned English, math, history, and geography, usually from European American teachers. Many of these adults believed they were helping Indian children. They tried to be kind. Others were cruel. Almost all the teachers taught the children that Indian ways were foolish and wrong.

The children spent most of their time working, not learning. Without student labor, the schools would not have had enough money to stay open. At some schools, even young children worked for hours almost every day.

Flandreau Indian School. At many boarding schools, girls prepared much of the food the students ate.

School superintendents believed that this work taught the children skills they would use as adults. Girls were expected to become servants or housewives. So they learned to sew, wash clothes, cook, and clean. Boys plowed fields and grew crops. They repaired harnesses, set up printing presses, and built furniture and houses.

Chemawa Indian School, 1882. Boys try out their blacksmithing skills.

Chilocco Indian School. Miss Robertson's class works in the school's vegetable garden. Such labor helped provide food and prepared the children to work for European Americans in the summer.

Many children also worked for European American families during the summer. This was called outing. Outing was supposed to help students practice their work and see how European Americans lived. Some students enjoyed leaving school and earning money. Others were treated badly. One girl wrote that her employer "always calls us Dunce, careless, lazy, ugly, crooked . . ."

Although the children worked hard, they often went hungry. The boarding schools did not have enough money for good food. Sometimes the food was spoiled. At Chilocco Indian School, one girl remembered there was "now and then a little mouse in your milk pitcher, a little dead mouse. And in the hardtack [crackers], if you'd crack 'em open . . . there'd be a few little worms in there."

Carlisle. Children eat chicken and corn in the dining hall. The food at Carlisle was more plentiful and nourishing than at many schools because Richard Henry Pratt convinced the U.S. government to provide the same food soldiers received.

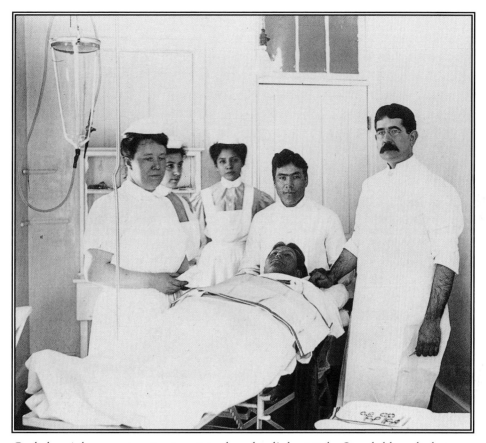

Carlisle. A boy receives treatment in the school's hospital. Six children died at Carlisle in the school's first year alone.

Because the schools were often crowded and dirty, many children got sick. Hundreds suffered from an eye disease called trachoma. Some went blind. The children also caught influenza, tuberculosis, and measles. Many died at the schools or soon after returning home.

Students also suffered from homesickness. Most boarding school superintendents believed that the children should not see their families. Students who went home during the summer might return to their people's ways. Some schools did not allow children to visit their parents for many years. But parents and children stayed in touch by writing letters. This contact helped the children remember that they were part of a family and community that cared about them.

Two boarding school students enjoy a rare visit home to the Fort Yuma Reservation in Arizona.

The children also turned to each other. Many had never met Indians from other nations or tribes. They built friendships that lasted their entire lives. Children wrote notes in Native languages so that the teachers couldn't read them. They made up funny names for mean teachers. They stole food to share and made nighttime less lonely by telling stories from home. When Basil Johnston's friends were supposed to be sleeping, one would cup his hand in his armpit and make rude noises "such as one would hear in a horse barn." Soon every boy in the room would join in, giggling.

Stewart Indian School. A moment of fun on a sunny day

Friendships helped the students have some good times. The schools often had sports teams. Girls could play basketball. Boys joined football, basketball, and baseball teams. Success in athletics made the children proud to be Indian.

Pierre, about 1925. The school's first girls' basketball team

Chilocco. Some of the actors in a play called Brave Heart *wore costumes that imitated traditional clothing.*

Many schools also had bands and choirs in which students could play and sing. Some schools put on plays. Students were sometimes allowed to spend an afternoon in town or go to a school dance.

Still, many children could not stand boarding school. They wanted to go home to see the places they knew and the people they loved. So they ran away. But running was dangerous. During the winter, some students froze to death. Others were caught and returned to school. Runaways might be locked in basements for weeks, beaten, or forced to do hours of extra chores. In spite of these punishments, many children ran away again and again.

Three runaway Wyandot girls are driven back to their school in 1901.

Haskell, early 1900s. The school's youngest children pose for a portrait.

The children also found ways to fight back. At the Haskell Institute in Kansas, students cut off the school's electricity. Then they rioted, damaging buildings. At Fort Mohave, kindergartners used a log to break down a door so their classmates could escape a locked room.

Children also resisted in smaller ways, too. They broke rules, sneaked out at night to meet friends, or spoke their own language. Acts like these helped them remain proud in a place where almost every adult wanted to destroy their pride.

*Carlisle. Students from several nations graduated in 1891. Henry Standing Bear,
who is also pictured on page 14, sits second from the left.*

After the Boarding Schools

The white man brought, you might say,
a new order of nature. . . . To survive,
we had to do things we never did before.
—Albert Yava, a Hopi student at Keams Canyon
Boarding School

Most children stayed at boarding school for about four years. Some stayed as long as ten years. But because doing chores was more important than learning at most schools, few students passed beyond sixth grade. By age eighteen, most left to look for a job or go home. Some found that they had learned a few helpful skills. For example, most former students could speak English, which helped them communicate with European Americans.

Gertrude Simmons, whose words appear on page 15, became a teacher at Carlisle. She later realized that she wanted to reclaim her Dakota heritage. She took a new name—Zitkala-Sa, meaning "Red Bird"—and worked to help Native Americans as a writer and lecturer.

Many students who went back to their reservations were happy to return to the families and communities they loved. For Carl Sweezy, an Arapaho student at Carlisle, "it was good to come back . . . to hear Arapaho spoken and to take part in Arapaho ceremonies and eat Arapaho food."

Others had a hard time coming home. The schools had prepared students for jobs that often did not exist on the reservations. Some students had forgotten their people's language. A few found that their feelings about home had changed. "When I left the Navajo country years before, I felt heartbreak," remembered Irene Stewart. "Now [after coming back] I was disappointed in it."

Chauncey Yellow Robe, who is also pictured on page 14, visits his father on the Rosebud Reservation in South Dakota in the late 1890s.

Some students did not go home at all. They had been taught for years that their people's traditions were bad, and they felt uncomfortable going back to the reservations. So they found jobs on farms or in towns. Some were hired by boarding schools to work as teachers, cooks, or caretakers.

These former students at All Hallows, an Indian boarding school in Canada, found work as servants.

Carlisle, 1908. In his best football season at Carlisle, Jim Thorpe scored 198 of the team's 504 points.

Jim Thorpe, a Sac and Fox Indian, was a boarding school student who became famous among both Indians and European Americans. An amazing athlete, Thorpe was the captain of Carlisle's football and basketball teams. He won two gold medals at the 1912 Olympics and later played professional football. Some people have called him the greatest athlete of the 1900s.

Carlisle, 1917. The school's last graduating class

During the 1920s, the American government began to respond to Indian criticisms of the boarding schools. Some European Americans realized that taking Indian children from their homes was wrong. During the mid-1900s, most of the boarding schools were closed. Instead, more day schools were opened on the reservations, where students could stay with their families.

Only a few Indian boarding schools are still open for older students who want to attend special programs. These schools aim to preserve Native traditions and languages, not destroy them.

The boarding schools changed the lives of many Indian people. But they did not succeed in their goal of destroying Indian culture forever. Former students, their children, and their grandchildren are working to undo the damage the schools caused. They are making sure that their people's stories and traditions are never forgotten.

Sherman Indian High School, 1996. Members of the intertribal student government show their pride to Ojibwe photographer Dorothy Grandbois.

Understanding Historical Photographs

Part I: What We Can't See

Have you ever heard the saying, "A picture is worth a thousand words?" Historical photographs hold many clues about how life was lived in the past. For example, study the details in the photograph of girls baking on page 21. How is the stove different from a modern stove? How are the girls' clothes and shoes different from those that modern children wear?

You can learn many things about life at an Indian boarding school from the photographs in this book. But when you study a historical photograph, it's important to think about more than just what you see. Ask questions about the things you *can't* see. Who took the photograph? Why? Does the photograph show people acting freely, or are they posed? Was the photograph created to show a certain point of view or to make viewers feel a certain way?

Photographers who visited the Indian boarding schools were usually invited or hired by school leaders. The photographers' job was to take pictures that showed how successful the schools were at changing Indian children. School leaders sometimes used the photographs to raise money. For example, at Carlisle, Richard Henry Pratt often had photographs taken of children before and after their arrival, such as those on page 14. Pratt showed these pictures to wealthy European American donors. He wanted to prove that his school turned Indian children into children who looked very much like European Americans.

To help you think more about the photographs in this book, try the activity below.

1. Study the photograph on page 19 of boys at Albuquerque Indian School. Have the children in this photograph been posed to look a certain way? How can you tell?

2. Draw a line down a piece of paper to make two columns. In the left column, make a list of things you see in the photograph. Your list might include things such as "uniforms," "boys in rows," and "American flags."

3. Next, try to think of reasons why a boarding school leader might ask a photographer to include each of these things in the photograph. For example, what are the American flags meant to show about this school's students? In the right column, write down these possible reasons.

4. Share your list with the other members of your class. Working together, write a short paragraph that describes the message you think this photograph was meant to send.

5. Follow these steps again to study other boarding school photographs in this book, such as those on pages 23 and 32.

Part II: Missing Pieces

You've learned that most boarding school photographs were created to prove a point. Their purpose was to show Indian children in a way that would make the schools look good to European Americans at the time. So the pictures tell only part of a complicated story. School leaders and photographers ignored or hid anything that might make the schools look unsuccessful or cruel.

Other parts of the boarding school experience could not be photographed. If an event such as a fire happened suddenly, there might not be time to record it with a camera. More importantly, Indian children had private lives that the schools, for all their power, could not reach. The close relationships children shared with their parents could not be captured in a photograph, except at the rare times when a parent was able to visit. We know about that closeness from the families' letters and stories, not from boarding school photographs. The friendships children built with each other appear in photos in only certain ways. We see activities like playing sports and acting in plays. But we don't see children laughing at a secret joke, telling stories at night, or comforting a frightened brother or sister.

When you study historical photographs, it's important to understand that they may not tell the whole story of a time or place. Reading about an event can help you get a more complete picture. So can talking to people who were involved. Follow the steps below to get a sense of what's missing from the photographic record of the Indian boarding schools.

1. Draw a line down a piece of paper to make two columns. In the first column, list some experiences described in the text of this book that do not appear in photographs. For example, your list might include calling a teacher a funny name (page 27) or being punished for speaking an Indian language (page 17).

2. Try to think of reasons why a photographer might not have taken pictures of these experiences. Would children be more likely to laugh at their teachers among themselves rather than out in the open? Would a photograph of children being punished make the school look bad? In the second column, write down these possible reasons.

3. Share your list with your classmates. How many parts of boarding school life did you find that do not appear in photographs?

4. To make your list even longer, read some of the books and visit the websites listed on pages 45 and 46. Perhaps you or your teacher know of someone who went to an Indian boarding school or has family members who did. Invite this person to visit your class and answer your questions about boarding school life.

5. If you can't find a visitor to speak to your class, your teacher can help you write a letter to the government of an Indian reservation in or near your state. In your letter, explain that you would like to learn more about the history of the boarding schools by writing to a former student or the descendant of a student. If you receive a reply from a person willing to write to your class, send a polite letter with your questions. Be sure to thank your correspondent for taking the time to write to you.

Resources on the Indian Boarding Schools

Child, Brenda J. *Boarding School Seasons: American Indian Families, 1900–1940.* Lincoln, NE: University of Nebraska Press, 1998. For adult readers. Through a study of letters written by students, parents, and officials at Haskell and Flandreau, an Ojibwe scholar examines the close bonds between families and the schools' effect on them.

Grutman, Jewel H., and Gay Matthaei. Illustrated by Adam Cvijanovic. *The Ledgerbook of Thomas Blue Eagle.* New York: Lickle Publishing Inc., 1997. This fictionalized picture book takes the form of the notebook of a Dakota boy at Carlisle. Thomas uses art and words to tell about his life before and after his arrival at school.

Harper, Maddie. *Mush-Hole: Memories of a Residential School.* Chicago: LPC/InBook, 1993. An Ojibwe woman describes her boarding school experiences and her struggle to overcome the negative training she received about Indian culture.

Hungry Wolf, Beverly. *Daughters of the Buffalo Women: Maintaining the Tribal Faith.* Surrey, BC: Canadian Caboose Press, 1997. A Blackfeet author shares stories of boarding school and reservation life, as told by her mother and other elder women of her tribe.

Johnston, Basil H. *Indian School Days.* Norman, OK: University of Oklahoma Press, 1989. An Ojibwe writer tells the story of his years at a Catholic school for Indian boys in Ontario, where friendship and a strong sense of humor helped students remain united and proud. Though written for older readers, Johnston's book contains many stories that would appeal to elementary readers.

Rappaport, Doreen. *The Flight of Red Bird: The Life of Zitkala-Sa.* New York: Dial, 1997. This biography for older readers features many long excerpts—including descriptions of boarding school life—from the writings of Zitkala-Sa, the Dakota author and activist whose photograph appears on page 34.

Sterling, Shirley. *My Name Is Seepeetza.* Toronto: Douglas & McIntyre, 1992. Based on the author's own experiences, this novel is shaped in the form of a diary of a Salish Indian girl who is renamed Martha Stone at a Canadian boarding school in the 1950s.

Websites
<http://home.epix.net/~landis/>
This detailed site features photographs, stories, and histories of students who attended Carlisle. Here you can read passages from the student newspaper, learn more about Jim Thorpe, and take a virtual tour of the school grounds.

<http://www.nps.gov/alcatraz/tours/hopi/hopi-h1.htm>
A historian from the Hopi Cultural Preservation Office tells the story of the Hopi men who endured arrest and imprisonment at Alcatraz rather than send their children to boarding school.

New Words

boarding school: a school where children live

European American: an American whose ancestors came from Europe. European Americans are often called "white."

mission school: a school where children are taught a new religion along with other subjects

outing: sending students out to work during the summer

reservation: a portion of land set aside by the American government for an Indian nation

superintendent: a person who runs a school

trachoma: an eye disease that sometimes causes blindness

treaty: an official agreement between nations

Index

Time Line

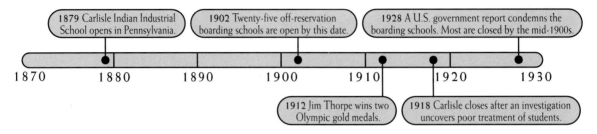

1870 — 1880 — 1890 — 1900 — 1910 — 1920 — 1930

1879 Carlisle Indian Industrial School opens in Pennsylvania.

1902 Twenty-five off-reservation boarding schools are open by this date.

1928 A U.S. government report condemns the boarding schools. Most are closed by the mid-1900s.

1912 Jim Thorpe wins two Olympic gold medals.

1918 Carlisle closes after an investigation uncovers poor treatment of students.

About the Author

Holly Littlefield has been a columnist, a waitress, a manuscript reader, a high school English teacher, and a volunteer counselor for runaway teens. She is currently teaching at the University of Minnesota. She lives in Minneapolis with her husband and two sons. This is her eighth book for children.

"When I look at the American government's attempts to separate Indian children from their families and cultures," she says, "I feel horror and disbelief. But I also pay tribute to the children, their parents, and their communities. Through strength and love, they worked to resist a system that was meant to destroy them."

Acknowledgments

The publisher gratefully acknowledges the use of quotations from: Paul Dyck, "Lone Wolf Returns . . . To That Long Ago Time." *Montana: The Magazine of Western History* 22 (January 1972), back cover, pp. 7, 13; Frank Mitchell, *Navajo Blessingway Singer.* Tucson, AZ: University of Arizona Press, 1978, p. 12; Clyde Ellis, *To Change Them Forever.* Norman, OK: University of Oklahoma Press, 1996, pp. 15 (top), 19; Zitkala-Sa, "Impressions of an Indian Childhood," *Atlantic Monthly* 85 (January 1900), p.15 (bottom); John Rogers, *Red World and White.* Norman, OK: University of Oklahoma Press, 1996, p. 16; Basil H. Johnston, *Indian School Days.* Norman, OK: University of Oklahoma Press, 1988, pp. 18, 27; *The Red Man* (September 1891), p. 23; K. Tsianina Lomawaima, *They Called It Prairie Light.* Lincoln, NE: University of Nebraska Press, p. 24; Albert Yava, *Big Falling Snow.* Santa Fe, NM: University of New Mexico Press, 1978, p. 33; Althea Bass, *The Arapaho Way.* New York: Clarkson N. Potter, 1966, p. 34; Irene Stewart, *A Voice in Her Tribe.* Socorro, NM: Ballena Press, 1980, p. 35. The photographs in this book are reproduced through the courtesy of: National Archives, pp. 1 (NWDNS–75–EXP–1D) (detail), 2 (NRE–75–PI(PHO)–7), 5 (NWDNS–75–L–3D), 8 (111–SC–95986), 12, 15 (NRFF–75–47–GLASS–107) (detail), 17 (NRE–75–PI(PHO)–2), 18 (NWDNS–75–EXP–2B), 19 (NRG–75–AISP–10), 22 (NWDNS–75–LP–1–23), 23 (NRFF–75–47–GLASS–107), 27 (NRHS–75–CARSN–DEC–048–8), 28 (NRE–75–PI(PHO)–11), 29 (NRFF–75–47–GLASS–1 (27)); Joslyn Art Museum, Omaha, Nebraska, p. 6; Cumberland County Historical Society, pp. 7 (detail), 9, 10, 14 (both), 16, 20, 24, 25, 33 (detail), 37, 38; Mennonite Library and Archives, Bethel College, North Newton, Kansas, p. 13; South Dakota State Historical Society–State Archives, p. 21; Arizona Historical Society Library, p. 26; National Museum of the American Indian, Smithsonian Institution, pp. 30 (N27364), 39 (P26523); Kansas State Historical Society, p. 31; U.S. Army Military Research Collection, Carlisle Barracks, Pennsylvania, p. 32; Photographic Archives, Harold B. Lee Library, Brigham Young University, Provo, Utah, p. 34 (P–MSS299); Smithsonian Institution, National Anthropological Archives, p. 35 (NAA–53328); National Archives of Canada/C–56774, p. 36. Front cover: National Archives (NRG–75–AISP–10). Back cover: National Archives (NWDNS–75-EXP–2B) (detail). Map on p. 11 by Tim Seeley, © 2001 by Carolrhoda Books, Inc.